I0755989

FINISHING LINE PRESS
www.finishinglinepress.com

HE DANCES IN HIS WHEELCHAIR

poems by

Charles Becker

Finishing Line Press
Georgetown, Kentucky

HE DANCES IN HIS WHEELCHAIR

ISBN 979-8-89990-405-9 First Edition

ACKNOWLEDGMENTS

Versions of some of these poems were previously published in literary journals, anthologies, chapbooks, or books. Thanks to the editors.

Friends My Poems Gave Me: "This First"; "We Can Begin"; "The Portrait and the Artist"; "The Artist and the Model"; "How We Run"; "People Who Ride the Bus"
Dodging Bullies: "In Our Hood"
Passager Journal: "Trees Out West"

Publisher: Leah Huete de Maines
Editor: Christen Kincaid
Cover Art: Charles Becker
Author Photo: Charles Becker
Cover Design: Elizabeth Maines McCleavy

Order online: www.finishinglinepress.com
also available on amazon.com

Author inquiries and mail orders:
Finishing Line Press
PO Box 1626
Georgetown, Kentucky 40324
USA

Contents

For Aubry and his differently abled brilliance

THIS FIRST

Days
back then
my early loves
so young
they surrounded
and changed me
even as I thought
I knew what I was doing
they, with Nebraska and hippie
smiles in tow
flawed lifelines across their palms
stunned outlooks
changed the future
by needing me.
Each moved closer
one after another
taught me to square dance
cooked our starchy dinners
played Scrabble
chanted with healers
drove to Mexico for the meds
and tried to lose
the virus haunting
their bodies
everyone
I held their hands
they held my heart
and then they died.

These days
I remember love
when he prods and pinches
shakes or shocks
holds and hushes me
from his wheelchair.

I dream a hibernation
sleeping away the wants
and winter hunger
learning a second spring.
It looks like tulip trees in April
aimless ochre poppy fields
jacaranda purples leaping
from the sky
it feels like two men
in bright light
burning off the early
May fog
paying tribute to cool
spoken mornings.

Most days
now
while I push too fast
too slow
he pumps with his arms
races downhill
laughs at my worries
throws his head back
and upper body dances
to the rhythm of Al Green
in the middle of the sidewalk.
I learn
once again
how love feels
if I tell someone
dreams just happen
naturally
when they're safe
and we can finally practice
writing poems
together

his flowing pure as breath
and mine
wrenched gently
so purposefully
from my hands
onto the waiting pages.

WE CAN BEGIN

Not so much because he likes
getting cards
or I like sending them
but because early on
he helps me
remember the reason we do
my heart and the way it hums
when not alone
turns over sounds
meant to be heard
by another doing the same.

For now it is his hands
I want
muscular and sure
like the full moon and stars
above his house.
When I ask
he reaches across the table
through our years
to begin this work
we do together.

We search for each other
in bed, his smooth
freckled skin foreshadows
saints and Valentines smiling
from the bedroom sky.
I listen to his stories
fluent and true
as they fly from his lips
into the open, evening envelope.

I know
they are not for me
but join him
to the world
and his desire
to be like
everyone else
finding their way
mobile
into the writing
of a life.

We pause for my turn
and I inhale to tell him
everything I know
how it is the quiet space
between thought words
the pause
before we speak
the closed eyes
alongside a smile
the soft beneath our kiss
all this
without needing to stand
gives a love poem
its real chance
for meaning.

THE PORTRAIT AND THE ARTIST

Night steeps above
Palm Springs swimming pools
aware of its own cobalt kindness
as pebbles, pink flamingoes, lilies
fall asleep. I sit in darkness
hearing crickets and occasional birds
until a harvest moon
rises lucid, loving cut grass below.
I can see its double
running the water's face
while a stucco house rests behind me.

My portrait of him looks
the way I want now
lines and shades settle
into the canvas
as my eyes
scan his perfect symmetry.
Here are the red
undertones of flesh
the square tapering
of shoulders
to his waist
foreshortening
of outstretched fingers
triangular knuckles
wrists made powerful
by the grip of his crutches
or push against his wheels
left hand larger
than his right.
Blacks and dark blues
in his hair
meet at the temples
bordered by patches white
as senior moments
and his eyes

staring
into mine
become brown
rich like chocolate
made with yellows
and greens
of Bayou cane sugar.
My painting is so alive
I start to confuse
who I am
with the portrait
I created. I remove
my thin shirt, lie flat
face pressed
against the cool
blades of winter grass.
Here I can climb
back into my own skin
before getting lost
forever in the study
of his.
Sanded mud squeezed
between my thumbs
drips smooth
onto the air molecules
of my breathing
and its warm mouthfuls
centering me
before I whisper
into bed
beside him
where practice will tend
finally
to my own drawings
dreamed.

THE ARTIST AND THE MODEL

Back home again
a cat's silhouette sits
by our upstairs window
trumpet flowers
hang yellow
in full June moonlight
while ocean air flutters
palm fronds
above the rooftop
and petals, pink ovals, tumble
from rose trees outside the door.

Sometimes at night
I hold him
as a question to answer
or idea repeated
over and over
so I won't forget
with his strong forearms
drawing us
toward a life
of luminescence
like the salty humid showering
of star-gazer lilies
planted close around the walkway.

Last
winter
we had rain
and spiders slipped soundlessly
out of sight
scurrying sideways
then underground through cracks
in the sidewalk.
He cursed those wet
web-like surfaces
always a threat to rubber tips

on walking sticks
propelling
and guiding
him to destinations
outcomes
where
if he fell
he climbed right
back up
furious
and ashamed of being seen
vulnerable
diminished.

Tonight
he turns
in bed
but does not wake up.
He's the one
I always saw
even when silence raged
tsunamis curled whitewater
and the eye of Rapture
stared at my loneliness.
I knew his Creole
profile
the scars
on his legs
and feet
long before
I learned them
with my fingers.

Gently
near the hour
he vocalizes
and seems to smile

invite me
mid-dream.
The moon
now kneeling
looks ready to move
into a higher sky
and I, too, can follow
into the acceptance
of kind
restfulness.

HOW WE RUN

He is Jupiter and Saturn
I, the stars between
he, the body's cells and soul
I, the constant heartbeat.
He is the words and the context
I, the musician
and instrument's notes
together we shape
and by necessity adapt.

Today, like other days
we stare out the window
watching weather
and people wander by.
I try to give names
to things we can't foresee
he writes about them
as if we can. I know him now
by his rants and prayers
letters and journals
where he dreams unedited
unafraid
out loud. I smile
at the differently
abled
authority
of his printed voice.
Love, like muscled hands
pushing through a crowd
touches my shoulder
surprises me always.
It offers itself
when I'm not looking
gropes and fondles
cries to be fed
prods and wallows
then smiles innocently

showing its teeth
just before we kiss.
He knows
it is in bed
he, becomes enabled, equal
I, disarmed
and charmed.
I am the ocean
he, mountains and desert
I am seeker and monk
he, prophet and priest
I am compassion
he, passion
I, trusting
he, reactive
I stumble
he survives
because
he
in a world
not made for him
each moment
chooses
resist to persist
perspire to inspire
and I
from an aging body
choose
to humbly remain
seated
and applaud
his every
step.

THROUPLE

I know you stare at him and wait for him all night, every night, vigilant and true. He reaches out often to touch you, make sure you're still there by his side of the bed, even as he holds my hand and whispers my name into the settled nighttime air. As you age, too, your back remains straight and strong, your core sexy-sleek, your essence erotic. He and I defer to you, depend on your masculine way of giving and being of service. When you joined us twelve years ago, mysterious and salacious as porn, I admit there was a tension among us at first. What did this mean about the future? Would you eventually take over and would we, the original two, be weakened, estranged from each other? It took time, like love and grief often do, to accept you. But now we'd be lost without you, the work and weight you carry, and the wholly accessed joy you bring to his face when he dances in your lap.

Who anticipates
living with a sports wheelchair
blends a family?

PEOPLE WHO RIDE THE BUS

Worn faces pressed
against each window
slick sweat at darkened scalps
dreams of rice and beans
corn tamales
settle in their stomachs
at Sunset and Vine
a bag lady smells
like newspaper, old shoes
used rouge
licks her fingers
and whispers teeth chips
into her hand
two drag queens wearing
5 o'clock shadows
platform heels
chatter lipstick gossip
into Tagalog
Hollywood High homeboys
bring it on
seize whole rows
and slouch
cock-proud of their badass
stolen iPods
the driver speaks to himself
non-stop
a seeing-eye dog stares at us
and sighs.

I no longer need to be good.
Tulips in my backyard
do not worry
their failure to win prizes
hummingbirds do not live in fear
of ever reaching paradise

grass, unknowing, grows green
in sunlight or in shade
it lives because it can
until it simply does not.

My love
no longer needs
to be perfect
when I hug him
in his wheelchair
a Monarch stirs inside
its cocoon
when he reaches up
hugs back
he claims an unbound
kingdom
I see him more each day
the way a penguin knows
its mate
through months of waiting
in the hungry Arctic dark
of promise.
He and I
now occupy
a coveted
front seat
the driver smiles
into his mirror
I am old
my love
sports spinners
on his wheels
and we
like the blind
ride free.

IN OUR HOOD

I want
no more lies
no sabotaging
self-talk
he's taught me
how to get
Black
when pushed
too far
by prejudice
and ignorance
just watch
how we take
his wheelchair
and get naked
to celebrate
the erotic
moves
of disabled sex
cerebral palsied
pleasures
and the success
of our bodies
sweating
youthful once again
then afterwards
laughing
to ourselves
I push, he rolls
outside
for some cool
air and enhanced
smell of our
night-blooming
jasmine, neighbors
walking by
smile approvingly

as they assume
I'm his caretaker
but I grin
nod back
and whisper
under my breath
No, he's my lover
and in fact
when we're
together
he walks
on water.

HE WANTS TO BE

like everyone else, like Huey Newton's brother
he preaches into the mirror, proud of kinfolk
ancestors, teachers from the motherland, each heart
he carries from the diaspora those who've been
homeless for so long he wants to lead them, be them
showcase their colors, bring their histories alive
like bright flowers along a powerful long stem
celebrating those who dared to share spoken truths

watch him sexy swoon to the rhythms of Jill Scott
book his library shelves with Walter Mosley reads
dance poised in his wheelchair not scorned in the spotlight
shined on Alvin Ailey's passion and legacy
yes, watch him wear those people well, become them all
abled and free as panthers learning their blackness
in the brightness of day from and for each other.

TREES OUT WEST

I have no angst to give you
no purgatory edge
I'm old, I've seen too much
and besides
in California we wear light
layers beneath our clothes
year round
no rain
so take, for example
cancer
and his oscillating
stalked cells
he patiently lives
among fronds
and the healing
smooth of palms
reaching for his wellness
few can imagine how
walking or running
with no more
than just arms
of hands
can only happen
in his most midnight
dreams
the thing is
he never complains
not even his eyes
because Angelinos
we're all about
the re-inventing or well
at least the acting as-if.
He knows
reclining in shade's
safety
it's not the words

you say
when praying
but the spin
comes within and without.
Every morning I trace
his face with a found twig
telling him he looks
more and more
like his motherlands
Senegal
Ghana
Cameroon
and he has work to do
stories to tell
because they push
they flow
through his blood.

HE IS

I see him now for who he really is, his lone wheelchair a throne
his crutches, like stilts, raising him up face to face staring down lies
he never wanted or asked for, wishing only to be like us.

ECHOLUCENT

At cardiac rehab they tell him those storms have stopped
he's reassured it is safe to walk outside again
his breathless fog has lifted, clogged clouds circulate free
and screened doors open pathways newly flush

he's reassured it is safe to walk outside again
two cushioned chairs inhabit him, red-chambered friends who chat
and screened doors open pathways newly flush
with dreams of beach umbrellas, pink toes imprinting sand

two cushioned chairs inhabit him, red-chambered friends who chat
gemmed cells refloat his future like collaterals rich in diamond mines
with dreams of beach umbrellas, pink toes imprinting sand
as echoes pump the light of open-hearted afternoons

gemmed cells refloat his future like collaterals rich in diamond mines
steeped healings pulse tamed bluebirds into one swirled cirrus horizon
as echoes pump the light of open-hearted afternoons
and puzzles search for pieces the way mistook clues go seek solutions

steeped healings pulse tamed bluebirds into one swirled cirrus horizon
his whole world now an everything gracing everything, nothing less
while puzzles search for pieces the way mistook clues go seek solutions
among woven rugs grounding this changed body, a summered waiting room

his whole world now an everything gracing everything, nothing less
each paced beat leaves him another and another and more others
while puzzles search for pieces the way mistook clues go seek solutions
at cardiac rehab they tell him those storms have stopped.

HE CLIMBS IN STARLIGHT

It is numinous lunar phosphorescent essence
and he begins to climb like a nimbus often will
hand over hand pulling itself closer to the source
of light but being human makes him slower, slower
going up than coming down, falling always likely
since his diagnosis he's not the same, taking big
chances caring less but the view from this much higher
is glorious sitting on branches leaned into nets
of leaves if he loses his grip when his heart might start
to sink again because just how many more times can
a heart fail wailing over the years it has bombed out
at romance, devotion, charity, friendship and doc
says it's a matter of function moving forward plus
the way he travels might slowly make it unstable
his body, though, keeps wanting to climb a little more
more, stretching, reaching the taller trees using their limbs
like arms and legs pushing him, holding him, lifting him
until the full moon is near enough to touch to feel
with the warm tips of his opened, extended fingers.

WE HAVE BECOME

I don't know
if this makes
any sense
but growing
older
I've learned
to leave
my body
when necessary
tending to him
in ER's
or ICU beds
his weathered
weakened
voice
hoarse
more thin
caretaking
is absolute
it's what I do
he
centers me
into a skill
no one can
teach
it
comes from
the memory
of our life
together
I might
resist
for
a moment
but later
surrender

celebrate
and respond
accordingly
I'm sure
soon enough
because
my own
self
still waits
I
will
rejoin
me
more ancient
a lot
more
worn
yet satisfied
I was there
for him
like
I promised.

TREES THIS NIGHT

Standing among
the palm trees
outside
his hospital window
I wave up to him
as the wind shoves
my body
twists me
sweeps through my brain
clearing it
of those thoughts
I no longer need
lost
I stumble
thrust my arms
around a smooth
trunk
and hold on
fearing
if I let go
I will blow away
forever
it bends and creaks
dares to push back
does not break
but grounds me
stretches my spine
and gets
how I need
to feel deeply
to be held
even as I am forced
to accept
the next time
or the next
when I look up
even higher

the he
the we
I always wanted
might be
gone.

Charlie Becker is a poet and visual artist who has been studying and guest-lecturing with the Community Literature Initiative (CLI) in Los Angeles for the past ten years. He has performed or read at open mics throughout Los Angeles and Pasadena, and his first book of poems and drawings, *Friends My Poems Gave Me*, was published in collaboration with World Stage Press in 2016. Charlie's poems tend to be about nature, art, friendships, or issues that impact the LGBTQ+ community and its seniors. Some of his poems have been published in *The Comstock Review, Quiet Diamonds (Orchard Street Press), Passager Journal,* and *The Dandelion Review*. Charlie's first poetry chapbook, *A Poem's Medium*, was published by Orchard Street Press in 2022. His second poetry chapbook, *Dodging Bullies*, was published by Finishing Line Press in 2023. Presently, he spends hours each day working in his garden, drawing, and wandering in the woods along wild-flowered trails to find inspiration for his word banks. Charlie lives with his partner, Aubry, in Laguna Woods, California.

www.ingramcontent.com/pod-product-compliance
Lightning Source LLC
LaVergne TN
LVHW090540110826
845146LV00003B/1205

* 9 7 9 8 8 9 9 9 0 4 0 5 9 *